A Look at

Jupiter

Ray Spangenburg and Kit Moser

Franklin Watts

A DIVISION OF SCHOLASTIC INC.
NEW YORK · TORONTO · LONDON · AUCKLAND
SYDNEY · MEXICO CITY · NEW DELHI · HONG KONG
DANBURY, CONNECTICUT

In memory of
Eugene Shoemaker
and for
Carolyn Shoemaker,
a stellar science team

Photographs ©: AKG London: 12; Art Resource, NY/Scala: 10; Astronomical Society of the Pacific: 79, 84; Brown Brothers: 54; Corbis Sygma/Jacques Tiziou: 74, 94; Finley-Holiday Films/NASA/JPL: 6, 52, 56, 61, 70; Liaison Agency, Inc.: 34 (N. Brown/Florida Today), 76 (Brad Markel), 33, 100 (ESA/NASA); NASA/JPL: 29, 31, 44, 45, 50, 82; Photo Researchers, NY: 77 (Julian Baum/SPL), 24 (Chris Butler/SPL), 86, 103 (David Ducros/SPL), 30, 109 (NASA/Science Source), 36, 53, 63, 65, 66, 68 (NASA/SPL), 46 (NAT Radio Astronomy Observatory/Astronomical Society of the Pacific), cover, 11, 13, 18, 38, 88, 104 (Science Photo Library), 8 (Jerry Shad/Science Source), 49 (J. Tennyson & S. Miller/University College London/SPL); Photri: 16, 20, 25, 27, 40, 48, 59, 80, 110.

The photograph on the cover shows Jupiter and some of its moons. The photograph opposite the title page shows Jupiter's Great Red Spot.

Library of Congress Cataloging-in-Publication Data

Spangenburg, Ray.
    A look at Jupiter / by Ray Spangenburg and Kit Moser.
        p. cm.—(Out of this world)
    Includes bibliographical references and index.
        ISBN 0-531-11769-3 (lib. bdg.)   0-531-16563-9 (pbk.)
    I. Jupiter (Planet)–Juvenile literature. [1.Jupiter (Planet)] I. Moser, Diane, 1944– II.
Title. III. Out of this world (Franklin Watts, Inc.)

QB661.S657 2001
523.45—dc21
                                                                        00-051357

Acknowledgments

To all those who have contributed to *A Look at Jupiter,* we would like to take this opportunity to say "thank you." Especially, a word of appreciation to our editor, Melissa Stewart, whose steady flow of creativity, energy, enthusiasm, and dedication have infused this entire series. We would also like to thank Sam Storch, Lecturer at the American Museum-Hayden Planetarium, who reviewed the manuscript and made many insightful suggestions. Also, to Tony Reichhardt and John Rhea, once our editors at the former *Space World* magazine, thanks for starting us out on the fascinating journey that we have taken—to Jupiter and many other places—during our years of writing about space.

Contents

Jupiter (upper left) shines brightly in the night sky.

Chapter 1

Early Views of Jupiter

When ancient astronomers looked up in the night sky, they saw thousands of twinkling stars. Most moved steadily across the sky, but a few behaved differently. Sometimes they sped up, and sometimes they slowed down. Sometimes they even seemed to move backward. The Greeks called these strange stars planets, which means "wandering ones."

One of these planets was Jupiter. The name "Jupiter" comes from Roman mythology. Jupiter was king of the Roman gods—the most powerful of all the gods. Clearly, Jupiter is an appropriate name for the largest and most powerful planet in our solar system.

Many other ancient people also tracked the movements of Jupiter. The Babylonians used the names Nibiru-Marduk and Udaltar to refer to Jupiter. They could predict the appearances of the planet over a span of more than 70 years. To Chinese observers, Jupiter was known as Mu xing. They charted the giant planet's path as well as the movements of its largest moon, Ganymede.

Modeling the Universe

In the early 1600s, an Italian astronomer named Galileo Galilei built an instrument that allowed him to get a closer look at the Moon and the known planets. When he turned his telescope toward the speck of light called Jupiter, he spotted something unexpected. Near the giant planet's edge, he observed three smaller points of light. As far as Galileo knew, no one had ever noticed these tiny glowing dots before. A few nights later, he spied a fourth tiny disk.

At first, Galileo thought the dots of light were stars. However, as he continued to watch them, he noticed that when Jupiter moved across the sky, so did the smaller specks. The tiny disks also seemed to change position around the planet. Eventually, Galileo realized that these objects were not stars at all. He had found four moons orbiting Jupiter!

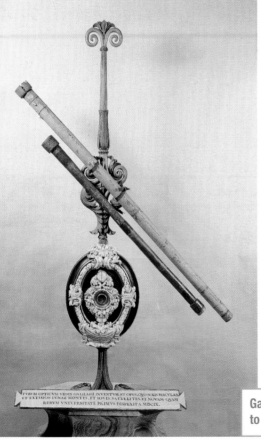

Galileo Galilei built this telescope and used it to observe the stars and planets.

Galileo Galilei discovered Jupiter's four largest moons.

This astounding discovery seemed impossible to most European astronomers and philosophers. It called into question the way they thought about the universe. For thousands of years, people had watched the Sun cross the sky and assumed it was orbiting Earth. Around 150, a Greek philosopher known as Ptolemy created star charts showing how the Sun, Moon, and planets move around Earth in perfect circles.

Ptolemy believed that Earth was at the center of the universe.

As time passed, some astronomers noticed problems with Ptolemy's theory. Its predictions did not always match their observations. To make the theory fit what people saw happening in the night sky, scholars made a series of minor adjustments to Ptolemy's original idea. These changes seemed to make the theory work.

By the 1600s, philosophers envisioned a universe of perfect circles, all revolving around Earth. The authorities of the Roman Catholic Church also supported this popular view. Galileo's observations of Jupiter's moons contradicted the way most people thought about Earth's place in the universe. After all, Galileo was suggesting that some bodies revolve around something other than Earth.

Polish mathematician Nicolaus Copernicus proposed that the Sun is at the center of the solar system.

Galileo was not the first person to question Ptolemy's theory. About 100 years earlier, a Polish scholar named Nicolaus Copernicus had suggested that the planets revolve around the Sun, not around Earth. He felt any model of the universe that needed so many adjustments was probably inaccurate. He knew that some ancient Greek and Roman philosophers had a different view of the universe. They thought the Sun was at the center of a solar system made up of planets and other objects. Copernicus embraced this alternate idea.

Because Copernicus's view was so controversial, his work was condemned by religious leaders and all but forgotten by most Europeans. Now, Galileo's discovery provided proof that Copernicus was right. People could look through Galileo's telescope and see the evidence for themselves. Jupiter's moons were moving around another planet, not around Earth.

Moving away from such a long-held principle did not come easily, and Galileo had to fight to get people to listen. The idea that everything in the universe revolves around Earth seemed so logical and "proper" to humans. Eventually, however, scientists began to realize that Galileo was right. Today we accept that the Sun is at the center of our solar system. Earth, and all the other planets, revolve around this glowing star.

In the last few decades, robotic spacecraft have allowed scientists to learn a great deal about our solar system. We now know that many planets have moons. Besides the four large Galilean moons, Jupiter's family includes at least thirteen other moons and a series of thin, tenuous rings.

Close-up views of Jupiter have shown us the planet's brilliant clouds. These images reveal bright white and yellow bands broken up by swirling bands of brown and deep-red. On one side of Jupiter, an enormous red storm, known as the Great Red Spot, spins angrily—as it has since long before Galileo first observed the giant planet with his telescope.

While modern scientists know much more about Jupiter than Galileo did, many of the giant planet's mysteries still remain to be solved. Hopefully, future missions to Jupiter and its moons will provide some of the answers we seek.

Jupiter's massive atmosphere swirls with fierce winds and ferocious storms, as shown in this color-enhanced view taken by *Voyager 1*.

Chapter 2

King of the Planets

Jupiter is the fifth planet from the Sun. Its orbit takes it 5.2 times farther from the Sun than Earth's orbit. Like Saturn, Neptune, and Uranus, Jupiter is a gas giant—a huge planet composed entirely, or almost entirely, of gas. Each of the gas giants has a low *density* and no solid surface.

Jupiter is entirely different from the rocky inner planets—Mercury, Venus, Earth, and Mars. It has no volcanoes, earthquakes, or impact *craters* and no mountains, valleys, or canyons. Jupiter is a rapidly rotating object with an enormous atmosphere composed mostly of hydrogen. Within this massive atmosphere, fierce winds and ferocious storms constantly rage, heave, and swirl.

As shown in this computer artwork, Jupiter is much larger than Earth. In fact, Jupiter could hold 1,408 objects the size of Earth.

Jupiter's commanding presence just beyond Mars and the asteroid belt has earned it the rank of "King of the Planets." It's so large that it could hold 1,408 objects the size of Earth. If you could crush all the planets into a fine powder and pour the powder into a hollow ball the size of Jupiter, there would still be plenty room left over. Its diameter

Jupiter and Earth

Vital Statistics

	Jupiter	Earth
AVERAGE DISTANCE FROM THE SUN	483,649,065 miles (778,357,721 kilometers)	92,955,808 miles (149,597,871 km)
DIAMETER AT THE EQUATOR	88,846 miles (142,984 km)	7,926 miles (12,756 km)
MASS	318	1.00
VOLUME	1,266	1.00
DENSITY	1.33	5.52
SURFACE TEMPERATURE	–240 degrees Farenheit (–151 degrees Celsius) at cloud tops	–94 to 130°F (–70 to 54°C)
PERIOD OF REVOLUTION (LENGTH OF ONE YEAR)	11.86 Earth-years	365.24 Earth days
PERIOD OF ROTATION (LENGTH OF ONE DAY)	9.83 Earth-hours	23.93 Earth-hours
MOONS	17	1

is more than 11 times larger than Earth's, and its mass is 318 times greater—more than two-thirds the total mass of all the planets in our solar system.

In fact, Jupiter is just about as big as a planet can possibly be—and still be a planet. If more material were somehow added to Jupiter, the planet wouldn't get bigger. It would shrink! The added material would cause the molecules to pack tighter, or compress—and the *volume* of Jupiter would actually get smaller.

Many young stars similar to our Sun are forming in this stellar "nursery," a dense cloud of dust and gas known as the Trifid Nebula.

Birth of a Giant Planet

Jupiter's beginnings trace back about 4.6 billion years. At that time, a giant, disk-shaped cloud of dust and hot, glowing gas began to form in our galaxy, the Milky Way. The cloud was one of many such disks, called *nebulae*, that have formed in our galaxy and in all the other galaxies throughout the universe.

Once the nebula formed, its *mass* began to collapse and condense, forming a brightly glowing ball of gas at its center. As the material at the center of the cloud became more massive, its *gravity* increased. This allowed the nebula to attract more matter to the tight, glowing ball. Finally, the pressure at the center of the nebula became so enormous and the heat became so intense that a process called *nuclear fusion* began to take place. As this reaction occurred, hydrogen gas was converted to helium gas and enormous quantities of energy were released into space. That is how our star—the Sun—was born.

Some of the material from the nebula continued to swirl around the newborn star. After about 100 million years, some of the dust and hot gases began clumping together. Small bits of dust stuck to each other, and these attracted more small particles. The clumps of material grew bigger as more and more particles were pulled in by gravity. These clumps were not big enough to form stars, so instead they condensed into *planetesimals*—the beginnings of what eventually became planets.

A small group of planets with rocky surfaces formed near the Sun. On these planets—Mercury, Venus, Earth, and Mars—most of the lighter gases, such as hydrogen and helium, were heated by the Sun and evaporated away. Farther away from the Sun, the gas giants— Jupiter, Saturn, Uranus, and Neptune—were able to retain the lighter

Science at Work: Is Jupiter a Failed Star?

By the late 1800s, scientists knew that Jupiter and the Sun were composed of similar materials. Hydrogen and helium—the main ingredients of Jupiter—are the same stuff that stars are made of. Some scientists wondered why Jupiter had become a planet while the Sun became a star. Those scientists did not know enough about how stars form to answer this question, but they developed a *hypothesis* that Jupiter might be a failed star.

As scientists learned more about stars and star formation, they discovered that stars are powered by nuclear fusion. For this reaction to take place, an object in space must have a tremendous amount of mass—seventy or eighty times more mass than Jupiter. It turns out that Jupiter was never a contender for stardom.

Does that mean that the scientists who developed the original hypothesis were foolish or stupid? No. They worked out a plausible explanation based on what they knew at the time. When new information became available, they drew new conclusions and developed new hypotheses. This is how science works.

gases. Because of their tremendous size and powerful *gravitational fields*, many smaller objects were attracted to the gas giants. These smaller bodies became the moons that orbit the big planets.

One of the most impressive planetary families in our solar system is located about 483,649,065 miles (778,357,074 km) from the Sun. It is composed of the enormous planet Jupiter, at least seventeen moons, and a set of thin, tenuous rings. Some of Jupiter's moons rival the planets Mercury and Pluto in size. Jupiter's family provides many intriguing places for scientists to explore.

Chapter 3

Exploring the Giant

From the time of Galileo to the 1970s, astronomers had only Earth-based telescopes for studying Jupiter. Because Jupiter is so far away and most of its moons are so small, scientists had trouble studying the planetary system. This difficulty ended when robotic spacecraft began visiting the outer solar system. Suddenly, we could clearly see the king of the planets and the members of its large family.

First Snapshots

For Jupiter, the new era of exploration opened with two spacecraft named Pioneer. Launched a few weeks apart, *Pioneer 10* and *Pioneer 11* arrived at Jupiter in the early 1970s. Suddenly, everyone everywhere knew about Jupiter's Great Red Spot and its banded cloud tops. Television news reports included stunning, colorful photos of the giant planet. The Pioneer missions changed the way Earthlings think about Jupiter.

Pioneer 10 was the first spacecraft to travel across the *asteroid belt*, and that part of the trip alone was an achievement. The idea of crossing the asteroid belt seemed incredibly hazardous to most people. They envisioned it to be something like a freeway—with objects whizzing by, traveling in wildly unpredictable paths. In reality, the thousands of space rocks—known as *asteroids*—that populate this region of space revolve around the Sun in orderly, predictable orbits.

There's plenty of space for a small spacecraft to pass safely through the asteroid belt, as shown by this artist's view from the surface of a large asteroid.

In this artwork, the Pioneer spacecraft's antennae look small and frail as it flies over Jupiter's stormy cloud tops and the Great Red Spot.

After studying the orbits of all the asteroids, engineers at the National Aeronautics and Space Agency (NASA) carefully mapped out the Pioneers' flight paths. *Pioneer 10* made its way through the asteroid belt without a mishap, and jauntily sailed on its way to Jupiter. *Pioneer 11* followed about a year later.

Pioneer 10 got the first close look at Jupiter as it passed by on December 3, 1973. In 1983, *Pioneer 10* became the first spacecraft to reach the edge of the solar system and it kept on going, but by 1997, the spacecraft's signal was too weak to follow.

On December 2, 1974, *Pioneer 11* passed within 26,700 miles (42,969 km) of Jupiter's cloud tops. The spacecraft sent the first photographs of Jupiter's polar regions back to Earth. Some of the images show a large white cap at the south pole. *Pioneer 11* also observed new movements in the Great Red Spot and captured close-up shots of Callisto, one of the moons first spotted by Galileo.

The two Pioneers collected vast quantities of information and captured dozens of images. The photos were really just teasers, though. Even better images would soon arrive from the next two spacecraft that NASA sent to the outer solar system.

Voyager: A Better Overview

When *Voyager 1* and *Voyager 2* arrived in Jupiter's neighborhood in 1979, the images they sent back were stunning. Not only did these spacecraft show close-ups of Jupiter like nothing anyone had seen before, they also showed the first true portraits of Jupiter's four big moons—Io, Europa, Ganymede, and Callisto.

Voyager 1 lifted off on September 5, 1977, and reached Jupiter on March 5, 1979. *Voyager 2* arrived at Jupiter on July 9, 1979. Then *Voyager 2* embarked on an exciting journey past Saturn, Uranus, and Neptune—taking advantage of an alignment of the outer planets that occurs only once every 189 years. This planetary line-up allowed *Voyager 2* to swing deftly from planet to planet like a ball racking up points on a pinball machine.

Together, the Voyager spacecraft helped scientists understand the complex forces that churn Jupiter's massive atmosphere. They also discovered three small moons—Metis, Adrastea, and Thebe—orbiting close to the planet. An even bigger surprise was the series of rings that the spacecraft detected around the planet.

Engineers carefully tested prototypes of the Voyager spacecraft to make sure the two Voyagers could survive in space. The dish antenna shown at the top of this image was used in flight to communicate with Earth.

When the Voyagers pointed their camera equipment at the Galilean moons, they captured images of active volcanoes on Io. *Voyager 2* even snapped a fast-action photo of an erupting volcano as it spewed molten sulfur into the blackness of space!

Galileo: Close Observer

The Voyager discoveries at Jupiter were so exciting that NASA decided to send another mission to Jupiter. This time the spacecraft, called *Galileo*, would focus all its attention on the giant planet and its four largest moons. The mission included a probe that would parachute into Jupiter's atmosphere and an orbiter that would tour Jupiter's inner neighborhood, taking close looks at all four Galilean moons and making occasional sweeps by Jupiter.

On October 18, 1989, *Galileo* was released from the Space Shuttle. Within moments, its booster rockets fired and the spacecraft was on its way. Because *Galileo*'s booster rockets were not powerful enough to take it all the way to Jupiter, the spacecraft made a detour. It headed in the opposite direction, toward Venus, so it could pick up some speed. *Galileo* swung past cloudy Venus and then zoomed around Earth twice, completing a maneuver NASA engineers call a *gravity assist.*

A gravity assist greatly reduces the amount of fuel a spacecraft needs by borrowing some energy from objects in space. As *Galileo* swung by Venus and Earth, it was pulled in by each planet's gravitational field. The spacecraft had enough momentum to prevent it from being pulled into orbit, but the force of the planet's gravity did bend the spacecraft's path, causing it to speed up. By taking advantage of the planets' gravitational fields, *Galileo* was able to slingshot around them and build up enough momentum and speed to reach Jupiter.

Galileo began its long journey to Jupiter on October 18, 1989, launched by astronauts from the Space Shuttle.

The gravity assist maneuver went just as planned, and by 1992, *Galileo* was headed in the right direction. As *Galileo* zoomed through the asteroid belt, it passed close to the asteroid Ida. Photos of the asteroid showed scientists something they hadn't expected—a moon! Since that time, scientists have discovered that Ida is not alone. Some other asteroids also have moons.

Finally, in December 1995, *Galileo* arrived safely at Jupiter. The orbiter's original tour of the moons and the giant planet was expected to last 23 months. It would complete eleven orbits and have ten close

This artist's conception shows *Galileo* arriving at Jupiter on December 7, 1995, just after flying by the moon Io, shown as a crescent to the right of the spacecraft.

In 1991, scientists realized that *Galileo* had a problem. Its High Gain Antenna, which was required for efficient communication between the spacecraft and scientists on Earth, failed to unfurl. The Galileo mission engineers tried all their technical magic, but the antenna failed to respond.

NASA engineers and scientists did not give up, however. The experts went to work and came up with a two-part plan. They devised a way to compress the large amounts of data *Galileo* would gather before it was transmitted to Earth. They also improved the receiving antennas in the Deep Space Network—a series of big radio antennas in Spain, Australia, and California that would receive communication signals from the spacecraft.

With these adjustments, *Galileo* could get the job done using just its Low Gain Antenna, even though this antenna operated at a much slower speed. Scientists soon found that by working around the problem, they could still accomplish most of the planned observations.

Huge dish antennas like these at the Deep Space Network site in Canberra, Australia, keep NASA engineers in touch with far-traveling spacecraft such as *Galileo*.

Research scientist Adriana Ocampo Uria was born in Colombia and raised in Argentina. Later, she moved to the United States. In 1973, while Ocampo Uria was still in high school, she began working for NASA's Jet Propulsion Laboratory (JPL) in Pasadena, California. Since that time, she has contributed her skills and expertise to several planetary missions, including the Galileo mission.

In the 1970s, Ocampo Uria worked on the imaging team for the Viking mission to Mars and helped plan the imaging of the Martian moons Phobos and Deimos. She also worked on the *Voyager 2* flight to Saturn. For the Galileo mission to Jupiter, Ocampo Uria worked as the science coordinator for the Near Infrared Mapping Spectrometer (NIMS)—one of the key instruments onboard.

Meanwhile, as a geologist, Ocampo Uria has also been active in the study of a fascinating crater here on Earth. The crater, located on the Yucatan Peninsula in Mexico, is known as the Chicxulub impact crater. Most scientists think that this crater marks the site where an asteroid hit Earth 65 million years ago. The impact is credited with causing the events that led to the mass extinction that killed the dinosaurs.

In 1991, while doing field research in Belize, Central America, Ocampo Uria discovered deposits of material the same age as those in the Chicxulub crater. She was able to show that the deposits had been ejected, or thrown up, from the Chicxulub crater at the time of the great impact. Since then, she has led several expeditions to study these rare deposits.

encounters with the four big moons—Callisto, Ganymede, Europa, and Io. In the end, *Galileo* accomplished far more than engineers expected. It orbited Jupiter for more than 5 years and had many additional opportunities to collect a wealth of data about the planet's moons.

Side Trip Stopovers

Two other missions have also visited Jupiter—both on the way to somewhere else. The spacecraft *Ulysses* passed through the Jupiter system in February 1992 on its way to make a series of passes over the poles of the Sun. More than 8 years later, the *Cassini-Huygens* spacecraft flew by. It was headed to Saturn to study the beautiful golden planet's rings and its large moon, Titan. Both missions were joint ventures of the European Space Agency and NASA.

Using a gravity assist trick similar to the one scientists had used with *Galileo*, these spacecraft took advantage of Jupiter's powerful gravitational field to speed them on their way. At the same time, the *flybys* allowed mission scientists to test their experimental equipment and collect some more information about Jupiter.

The idea of getting to the Sun by heading for Jupiter might seem strange, but it worked well for *Ulysses*. Looping past Jupiter gave the spacecraft the extra energy it needed to move into an orbit that passes

After its launch from the Space Shuttle, *Ulysses* flew by Jupiter in 1992, on its way to become the first spacecraft to circle the Sun over its poles.

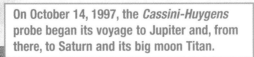

On October 14, 1997, the *Cassini-Huygens* probe began its voyage to Jupiter and, from there, to Saturn and its big moon Titan.

by the polar regions of the Sun. Even with Jupiter's assistance, *Ulysses* required the lift of the Space Shuttle and three upper-stage booster rockets to reach its target.

In December 2000, the *Cassini-Huygens* spacecraft visited Jupiter as it headed for Saturn. Jupiter's massive gravitational field provided the push the spacecraft needed to accelerate toward its final destination. While *Cassini-Huygens* was in the Jupiter neighborhood, scientists took advantage of a rare chance to observe Jupiter's powerful *magnetic field* from two different points at the same time. *Cassini-Huygens* collected data from one spot while the die-hard *Galileo* made similar measurements from a different position.

Jupiter's light-colored bands are known as "zones" and the giant planet's dark-colored bands are called "belts."

Chapter 4

Inside Jupiter

Jupiter's atmosphere is made up of hydrogen, helium, methane, ethane, ammonia, water vapor, and acetylene. This mixture of atmospheric gases would quickly kill most creatures on Earth, but there is no life on Jupiter.

When you look at a picture of Jupiter's cloudy atmosphere, you can see a series of colorful bands. Astronomers have traditionally called the light-colored bands "zones" and the dark-colored bands "belts." The North Tropical Zone—the region located about halfway between the equator and the north pole—has the brightest clouds. Scientists believe these clouds contain particularly large quantities of ammonia.

The dark-brown and orange bands near Jupiter's poles and equator contain large concentrations of organic molecules, such as ethane. They are turbulent wind channels that run parallel, but in opposite directions, around the planet's circumference. They move at enormous speeds—up to 335 miles (539 km) per hour.

Huge white and dark spots sprinkled across the cloud tops mark the site of hurricanes and cyclones that spin in enormous ovals. These powerful storms form between the bands of wind channels.

The Great Red Spot

One of Jupiter's most well-known surface features is the Great Red Spot. It is a gigantic anticyclone—a southern hemisphere storm with winds that swirl in a counterclockwise direction. It takes 6 days for the winds within the Great Red Spot to make a complete circular cycle.

Most hurricanes and cyclones on Earth last only a few days, but the Great Red Spot has been furiously swirling for hundreds of years. In 1664, the English scientist Robert Hooke (1635–1703) reported that he had seen "a spot in the largest of the three belts of Jupiter." Another astronomer, Italian-born Giovanni Domenico Cassini (1625–1712), reported seeing a large spot several times between 1665 and 1691. Then, mysteriously, no one else reported seeing it until 1878, when the sharp eyes

Italian astronomer Giovanni Cassini's many contributions to astronomy include observations of Jupiter's Great Red Spot.

of American astronomer Edward Barnard (1857–1923) spied it once again.

Why did astronomers lose sight of the Great Red Spot for two centuries? Scientists are not sure, but they have some theories. The super-sized storm may have been difficult to see with early telescopes. In addition, its visibility may have varied during the interval between its first discovery by Hooke and its rediscovery by Barnard.

In 1887, astronomers decided it was a feature that was there to stay, and they officially named it. At the time, no one was quite sure what the spot was. Some people thought it might be an enormous island. Others suggested that it might be clouds clustered around a huge mountain peak. Not until many years later did scientists realize that it is a gigantic, whirling, seething storm system.

The Great Red Spot is just one of the many spots visible on Jupiter, but most of the others come and go. While the Great Red Spot has changed somewhat in size and shape over the centuries, it has always remained an enormous, commanding presence. Today, the Great Red Spot is more than 8,500 miles (13,679 km) wide from north to south and varies between 14,913 and 24,955 miles (24,000 and 40,161 km) wide from east to west. It could easily swallow up two balls the size of Earth.

What gives the Great Red Spot its color? Some scientists believe that the clouds may contain large quantities of the element phosphorus, which is red or deep orange. Others believe the color may be caused by the presence of sulfur, which can also be orangish-red. Strangely enough, scientists who examined the results from the Voyagers' infrared spectrometer found no difference between the chemical composition of the Great Red Spot and the smaller white spots that appear and disappear all over the planet. No one is sure why.

Large quantities of phosphorous, or perhaps sulfur, may color the Great Red Spot.

At times, the Great Red Spot seems paler than its usual dark brick-red color. Sometimes the color does vary, but sometimes an optical illusion is at work. When the turbulent winds that flow outside the storm center are darker than usual, the color of the Great Red Spot seems lighter by comparison.

Some scientists wonder why Jupiter has only one red spot. They would like to know why there is no similar storm in the planet's northern hemisphere. They also are curious about why the anticyclone has continued to swirl so endlessly. The most likely explanation is the immense turbulence created when the winds in neighboring atmospheric bands move past one another at full gale force. Or perhaps the Great Red Spot is so huge that nothing can disrupt its movement.

Inside a Large Gas Ball

Below the clouds we see from Earth lies a layer of bright white clouds formed by crystals of frozen ammonia and frozen water. Together, these two cloud layers make up only a tiny fraction of the planet's bulk—about 1 percent of its *radius*, the distance from the tops of its clouds to its center.

The temperature at the top of Jupiter's clouds is a chilly –120°F (–84°C). But deeper inside the planet, it is much warmer. Just 35 miles (56 km) down, the temperature is reminiscent of balmy weather on Earth. At the center of the planet, the temperature reaches a sizzling 50,000°F (27,760°C).

Most of Jupiter's interior is composed of hydrogen. Hydrogen usually exists as a gas, but about 600 miles (966 km) below Jupiter's cloud tops, the tremendous pressure of the gases above turns hydrogen gas into a planet-wide ocean of liquid hydrogen. Even deeper—about

10,000 miles (16,093 km) below the cloud tops—the crushing pressure of the layers above transforms hydrogen into a substance known as metallic hydrogen. Some scientists believe that Jupiter may have a solid iron core at its center, but others think that no part of Jupiter is made up of solid material.

Chapter 5

Magnetic Personality

Walk into almost any kitchen, and you'll see a refrigerator covered with notes and pictures. These items are probably held in place by small, decorative objects that stick to the refrigerator door. If you look on the back of these small objects, you'll see what keeps them attached to the steel refrigerator door—magnets. Would you believe that a refrigerator magnet has something important in common with the planet Jupiter? Both are magnetic.

You can think of Jupiter as an enormous magnet. In fact, Jupiter's *magnetism* is one of the giant planet's most striking personality traits. Magnetism is a force that allows some objects to attract or repel other objects—even when they are not touching. Magnetism can also hold objects together when they are touching. The area affected by a magnet's attractive force is called a magnetic field.

Jupiter spins like a huge top. It completes one rotation, or spin around its axis, in less than 10 hours. That means a day on Jupiter is less than half as long as a day on Earth. Jupiter spins so quickly that the planet bulges out at its equator, making it look like a squashed ball. The planet's speedy spinning also causes its internal metallic hydrogen layer to act like an extremely powerful magnet. Jupiter's enormous magnetic field extends millions of miles into space.

Giant Area of Influence

The first spacecraft to visit Jupiter, *Pioneer 10,* created a map of Jupiter's magnetic field. The map showed that the size of Jupiter's magnetic field changes in response to pressures from *solar wind*—a stream of highly magnetic, electrically charged particles ejected at high speeds from the Sun's surface. The solar wind whizzes past Earth at 185 to 435 miles (300 to 700 km) per second.

When solar wind interacts with Jupiter's magnetic field, it creates a vast, invisible electromagnetic region called a *magnetosphere.* The size and shape of Jupiter's magnetosphere is

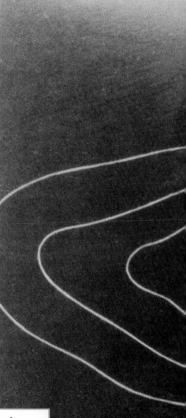

Jupiter's giant magnetosphere has an enormous region of influence. It stretches millions of miles across our solar system.

influenced by the Sun's cycle of activity. Most of the time, the magnetosphere has a blunt "nose" that points toward the Sun and a wide, fan-shaped tail that extends far beyond Pluto and Neptune. Jupiter's magnetosphere is the largest structure in the solar system.

While the spacecraft *Ulysses* was in Jupiter's neighborhood, it had a chance to study the magnetic environment around the big planet. The spacecraft also provided a "road map" of the various regions within Jupiter's magnetosphere.

Radio Broadcasts from Jupiter

Have you ever wondered how a radio works? How do the waves of sound from a blaring CD travel from a radio station to your home? Like visible light and *ultraviolet rays* from the Sun, radio signals are a form of *electromagnetic radiation*. They are produced at a frequency that we can hear. Each radio station broadcasts at a slightly different frequency. When your radio dial is tuned to the frequency used by your favorite station, you can pick up its signal.

Would you believe that scientists have found ways to tune into natural radio signals given off by the planet Jupiter? Jupiter's radio signals are not messages of the usual sort, though, and no intelligent beings are behind them. They are just "noise."

These signals are created when Jupiter's enormous magnetic field captures particles of solar wind as they travel through space. Lightning flashes and ferocious thunderstorms within Jupiter's atmosphere add to the static.

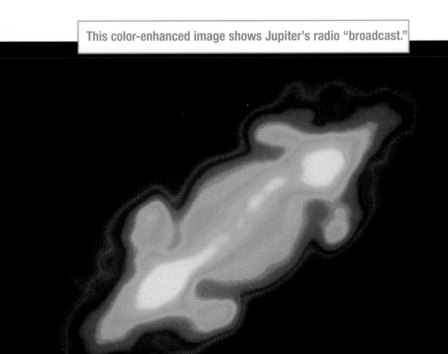

This color-enhanced image shows Jupiter's radio "broadcast."

The light we see is only one part of a range of waves known as electromagnetic radiation. On the short end of the spectrum are gamma rays, X rays, and ultraviolet (UV) rays. In the middle is visible light. On the other end of the spectrum are the long waves of infrared radiation, microwaves, and radio waves.

All these waves are invisible to humans. Yet, we can feel the heat of infrared radiation, and we know we have to protect ourselves from the UV radiation of the Sun. Many satellites carry instruments that can "see" the gamma-ray, X-ray, UV, or infrared radiation that comes from objects. In astronomy, these special instruments reveal aspects of the universe that are otherwise invisible or very faint.

Gamma rays are produced by nuclear processes, including fission, fusion, and radioactive decay. When astronomers observe gamma rays coming from the sky, they are able to locate objects that are extremely hot and are perhaps in the process of forming heavier chemical elements.

X-ray observations concentrate on objects in space that give off X-ray radiation—also near the short end of the spectrum. X-ray astronomy has unveiled new clues about the large-scale structure of the universe and has also explored such highly puzzling objects as *pulsars* and black holes.

UV detectors, on the other hand, look at UV radiation, just beyond visible light at the short end of the spectrum, but having a longer wavelength than either X rays or gamma rays.

Infrared radiation has longer wavelengths than visible light, but shorter than microwave radiation or radio waves. All objects with a temperature higher than absolute zero emit some infrared radiation, and some very cool stars actually give off more infrared than visible radiation. So, infrared astronomy is especially good for observing faint or cool objects in space.

The Electromagnetic Spectrum

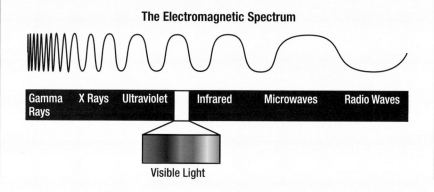

Visible Light

Ulysses traveled all the way to Jupiter to pick up a gravity assist so it could reach its unusual polar orbit around the Sun.

You probably wouldn't enjoy listening to Jupiter's crackling, hissing radio broadcasts, but scientists know that they can teach us a great deal. While *Ulysses* was visiting Jupiter, scientists used special equipment onboard the spacecraft to study the planet's unusual broadcasts.

Awesome Light Shows

When the energetic charged particles in solar wind interact with Earth's atmosphere, people living in the northern parts of Earth can see a colorful light show called aurora borealis, or the northern lights. Meanwhile, people living thousands of miles away can view a similar display. The southern light show is called aurora australis, or the southern lights. An *aurora* occurs when disturbances on the Sun's surface pump up the quantities of charged particles flung toward Earth.

Jupiter has incredible light shows that are even more stunning and more frequent that those on Earth. That's because energetic charged particles are always trapped in Jupiter's enormous magnetosphere.

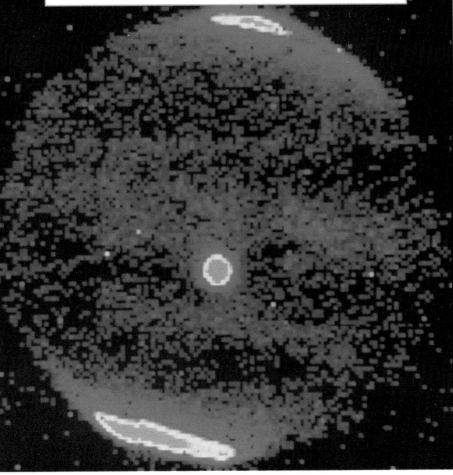

Jupiter's aurorae appear as yellow and red areas near the poles in this color-enhanced infrared map. (The red spot at the center is the moon Ganymede, reflecting infrared radiation from the Sun.)

This computer-generated montage combines a starry background and images taken by *Voyager 1* in 1979, including Jupiter and the Galilean moons (top to bottom) Io, Europa, Ganymede, and Callisto.

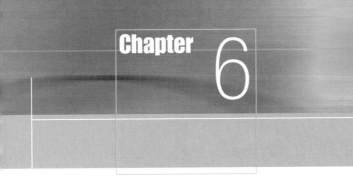

Chapter 6

Skinny Rings and Weird Worlds

Jupiter's bizarre weather, strange ocean of metallic hydrogen, and giant magnetosphere are truly amazing. But the planet's intrigue does not end there. The king of the planets also has a large family of mysterious moons. Four of these worlds are the Galilean moons discovered by Galileo Galilei in 1610 and explored by the spacecraft that bore his name. These moons are among the largest and most varied in the solar system—ranging from hot, volcanic exteriors to frozen ice fields. At least thirteen other moons round out the family. One is so small that you could jog from one side to the other in a couple of hours. Close to the giant planet hovers another fantastic feature—a set of thin, ghostly rings. These rings are so faint that they went unde-tected until 1979!

Rings and Things

For many centuries, astronomers thought that Saturn was the only ringed planet in the solar system. Then *Voyager 1* proved otherwise. As it flew by Jupiter, the spacecraft turned its camera toward an area just above the planet's equator and set the shutter for an 11-minute expo-sure. The scientists who planned this photo session wondered whether a ring just might exist there. Since the makeup of Jupiter is so similar to that of Saturn, they thought that perhaps the king of the planets had some faint rings.

Jupiter's rings are very difficult to photograph, but this simulation gives an idea of what they look like.

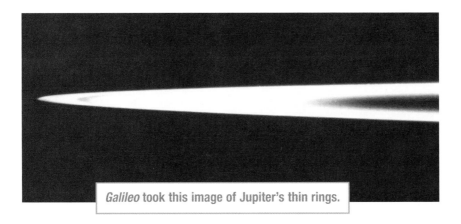

Galileo took this image of Jupiter's thin rings.

Images from *Voyager 1* proved that the scientists were right. The pictures clearly show a narrow band around Jupiter's middle. The band consists of a flattened main ring and a halolike, cloudy inner ring. A third, very faint outer ring also seems to appear in the Voyager images. In 1996 and 1997, images from *Galileo* showed that this outer ring is actually two nearly transparent "gossamer" rings. By the end of the Voyager mission, scientists knew that all four gas giants—Jupiter, Saturn, Uranus, and Neptune—have rings.

Now that astronomers know where to look, they can sometimes detect Jupiter's rings using high-definition, ground-based telescopes. These faint hoops look nothing like Saturn's vast rings. Jupiter's rings are very thin. The largest is only about 18 miles (29 km) thick.

Their composition is completely different too. Saturn's rings consist of icy chunks that range tremendously in size. Some are as small as grains of sand, while others are as big as boulders. As far as planetologists know, Jupiter's rings contain no ice. They are composed of dark-reddish soot-like material, dust, and fine particles from the many *meteoroids* that have collided with Jupiter's four small inner moons—Adrastea, Metis, Amalthea, and Thebe.

The larger particles produced by these high-impact crashes don't get caught up in the rings. Instead, they are captured by the moons' gravitational fields. Only tiny particles that have benn pulverized to a fine dust by the explosive impact and flung free of the moon become part of the rings.

Why do the tiny particles end up orbiting the planet as rings? The largest ones are held in place by Jupiter's gravitational force. However, as they rub against one another, they begin to erode into even smaller bits. Then they fall toward the planet. This process usually takes about 1,000 years.

Even though particles eventually fall out of the rings, the rings do not disappear. New chunks of rock and ice are constantly drawn toward the giant planet. Inevitably, many collide with the nearby moons, and new particles quickly replace those that fall out.

The Inner Moons

On the night of September 9, 1892, American astronomer Edward Emerson Barnard was observing Jupiter at the 36-inch (91-cm) refracting telescope at Lick Observatory on Mount Hamilton near San Jose, California. Nearly three centuries had passed since the Italian astronomer Galileo Galilei discovered the

American astronomer Edward Barnard discovered Amalthea in 1892.

The Man with Peerless Eyes: E. E. Barnard

Edward Emerson Barnard was born in Nashville, Tennessee, just before the Civil War broke out. His father died before Edward was born, and his family always had to struggle to put food on the table. When Edward was 9 years old, he was taken out of school and sent to work in a portrait studio. He worked there for the next 17 years.

During those years, Edward developed a keen interest in astronomy. He began observing stars, planets, and other objects as an amateur and showed his talent by discovering a *comet*. He eventually found a way to attend Vanderbilt University in Nashville, Tennessee, where he continued to study astronomy and was placed in charge of the college's observatory.

As a qualified professional astronomer, Barnard obtained a position at Lick Observatory. Although he was never strong in mathematics, his powers of observation were widely admired. At the telescope, he had a rare talent for noticing fine detail and recognizing what was significant.

In 1892, Barnard noticed a puff of gaseous material given off by a nova in the constellation Auriga. This was a strong clue that an explosion had taken place. Until that time, astronomers were not sure just what was taking place within a nova. That was the same year that Barnard discovered Jupiter's moon Amalthea.

Later, Barnard discovered craters and volcanoes on Mars. But he is probably best remembered for his discovery of a strange star. Although it was very dim, the star seemed to move incredibly fast across the sky. Surprisingly, "Barnard's Runaway Star" turned out to be one of the closest stars in the universe. It seems so faint because it is very small and relatively cool.

four largest moons of Jupiter, and no one had ever found another moon orbiting the king of the planets. Barnard's reputation as a keen observer stood by him that night as he caught sight of a tiny object very close to Jupiter's giant glow. He had discovered a fifth moon!

The new moon was closer to Jupiter than the four Galilean moons, and much smaller. As the moon's discoverer, Barnard intended to give it a name, but he never did. Some people still call it Barnard's *satellite*. However, French astronomer Camille Flammarion called it

This Voyager image shows tiny, red Amalthea—
one of Jupiter's innermost moons.

"Amalthea," the name of the mythological goat that nursed Zeus (the Greek counterpart of the Roman god Jupiter). That name stuck. It was the last moon of Jupiter discovered without the help of photography, and its discovery is a tribute to Barnard's sharp eyes.

Amalthea is shaped like a football, and its surface is pockmarked by impact craters. This moon's irregular shape has led scientists to believe that it broke away from a larger body when that object was struck by a meteoroid. Amalthea orbits sideways, with one end always pointing toward Jupiter. It speeds around the planet's giant circumference in just 12 hours.

Amalthea is the reddest object in the solar system. Its bright red color probably comes from dust cast off by the active volcanoes of nearby Io. As the reddish sulfur dust from Io's volcanoes spews into space, the particles are caught by Jupiter's gravitational pull and spiral toward the planet. On the way, some of them land on Amalthea. Like a bit of makeup on its outer skin, the red coloring gives Amalthea a rosy complexion.

If an astronaut could stand on Amalthea, he or she would see flashes of lightning traveling among Jupiter's cloud tops. At a distance of only 112,654 miles (181,300 km), the planet's giant face would fill most of the sky.

The tiny moons Metis and Adrastea orbit closer to Jupiter, on the outer edge of its main ring. Along with the larger moon Thebe, these two moons were discovered by the two Voyager spacecraft in 1979. The two worlds are truly petite. Metis is only 26.7 miles (43 km) across, and Adrastea is half that size—9.9 miles (16 km) in diameter. You could easily pedal that far on your bicycle.

According to calculations made by French mathematician Edouard Roche (1820–1883), if a moon gets too close to a planet, it will disintegrate. Roche calculated that if a planet and moon have the same density, this catastrophe will take place if the moon is closer to the planet than 2.44 times the planet's radius. This distance has become known as Roche's limit.

Interestingly, Metis and Adrastea both reside within this limit, and so do the rings of all four gas giants. That is why many scientists believe that the particles that make up planetary rings may contain the leftovers of disintegrated moons. But why don't Metis and Adrastea disintegrate? Some scientists believe that Roche's calculations did not consider the type of materials a moon is made of or the inherent ability of some materials to stick together. These factors could keep a moon from breaking up, even if it is very close to a planet. Perhaps that is why Metis and Adrastea can travel so close to the main ring, and inside Jupiter's two gossamer rings, without becoming part of them.

It is also possible that the moons are so small compared to the mass of the giant planet that they are not affected by Jupiter's *tidal forces*— the difference between the force of gravity on the near and far sides of an object. These tidal forces cause considerable stress on larger moons, such as Io, but do not seem to influence Metis and Adrastea. Nevertheless, Jupiter's gravity will someday pull these small, irregular moons out of their orbits. They will shatter into tiny bits as they fall toward the giant planet.

Between Amalthea and the volcanic moon Io roams Thebe, a roughly ball-shaped moon surrounded by a cloud of glowing sodium. Thebe is smaller than Amalthea—only about 61.5 miles (99 km) in diameter. The surface of this mottled, red moon is covered with large craters.

Thebe is closer to Io than any other world, and it could provide astronauts with a front-row seat from which to view the larger moon's dynamic geology. From the dark side of Thebe, explosions are visible as Io's volcanoes spit out hot, glowing lava. From the sunlit region of Thebe, illuminated ashes are visible along the larger moon's rim.

The Galilean Moons

The Voyager spacecraft gave scientists their first exciting close-up glimpses of Jupiter's four Galilean moons. They showed us that each moon is quite different, as if invented by a science fiction writer whose imagination had run wild. The story of the moons became even more gripping when *Galileo* returned to Jupiter's system to take a longer and much closer look at Io, Europa, Ganymede, and Callisto.

Land of Molten Lava

Of the four big moons, Io has the most stunning appearance. It looks like a giant pizza ball, covered with dripping cheese, steaming tomato sauce, and ripe black olives. Io is slightly larger than Earth's Moon. Of

This full-disk image of Io was composed from several pictures taken by *Voyager 1*. The circular, donut-shaped area in the center is an active volcano. The entire surface of Io is paved with lava that flows from vents or spews into space in explosive eruptions.

the four Galilean moons, it is closest to Jupiter and, it takes the most hits from asteroids and meteoroids as they fall at high speed into Jupiter's gravitational field.

However, volcanic craters—not impact craters—are Io's most prominent feature. Some eighty volcanoes rack the moon's surface with constant heaving as they spew molten sulfur into the blackness of space. So much geological activity takes place daily on Io that, by comparison, Earth seems sedate and placid.

Photos taken by the Voyager spacecraft show us that Io's volcanoes are violent and dramatic. They blast streams of molten material into space at speeds up to 2,300 miles (3,700 km) per hour. Also, since Io's weak gravity pulls on objects with only one-sixth the tug of Earth's gravity, the plumes from the moon's volcanoes spurt as high as 162 miles (260 km) into space!

At the time, however, scientists had no inkling of the frenzied pace at which Io performs. In 1995, the *Hubble Space Telescope*, an astronomical observatory that orbits in space above Earth's atmosphere, showed us that the action on Io is nonstop. From *Hubble*'s pictures, scientists could see that an enormous new volcano had formed in just the 16 years since the Voyager missions had visited Jupiter's neighborhood.

Exciting new close-ups also came from the *Galileo* spacecraft in the 1990s. Between the time the Voyagers left and *Galileo* arrived, the surface of Io had changed radically. Startling photos from *Galileo* revealed many new volcanic vents on the moon's surface, and even more plumes were spewing violently into space. Above some of the erupting volcanoes, a bluish glow appeared. In some places, huge power surges generated bright arcs of light above Io.

Galileo took this color-enhanced view of Io showing a jet of blue material being heaved into space by an active volcano. The inset (upper left) shows the eruption close up.

Images taken by *Galileo* also show a rash of glowing, red lava pools on Io's surface. Huge new lakes of molten sulfur lap against scorching hot shores, and new volcanic cones stud the satellite's face. In fact, Io has so many active volcanoes that the flowing lava has completely erased all signs of meteorite impacts.

Equipment onboard *Galileo* has shown scientists that Io's lava flows are incredibly hot—hotter than any eruption on Earth has been for billions of years. The heat from one vent was measured at 3,100°F (1,700°C)! No other body in the solar system has temperatures that hot, except the Sun.

What causes all this violent activity? Scientists don't know for sure, but their best guess is a combination of forces caused by Jupiter and nearby moons. Jupiter's mighty gravitational field creates a great deal of friction within Io's molten core. The pizza-faced moon is also affected by its neighbors, Europa and Ganymede. These two moons are caught in a tug-of-war that also pulls at Io. Locked in step with these moons, Io makes two trips around Jupiter for every one trip completed by Europa. In turn, Europa makes two trips around the giant planet for every orbit completed by Ganymede.

The tension among these bodies tortures Io's surface with enormous tides. As tidal forces shift Io's molten interior, the moon's pliable surface bulges as much as 328 feet (100 meters). All this stretching and pulling makes the inside of Io seething hot. As far as scientists know, this moon's strange and violent dynamics are unique in the solar system.

World of Icy Oceans

Europa is about the size of Earth's Moon, but the two satellites don't look much alike. The ancient, pockmarked surface of Earth's Moon is carved up by thousands of impact craters. Many of our Moon's craters date back to the beginning of the solar system. Europa, by contrast, has almost no craters on its sleek, icy surface. In fact, this satellite may have the smoothest surface in the solar system. Europa's smooth exterior is what geologists call a "young" surface.

Some geologic force has covered the ancient impact craters that once existed on Europa's surface. Scientists know that the early solar

The long, dark lines in this image taken by *Galileo* are cracks in the crust of the ice-covered world Europa. Some of these cracks are up to 1,864 miles (3,000 km) long.

system was a free-for-all, with new-born planets, moons, asteroids, meteoroids, and comets slamming into each other as they careened through space like bumper cars at an amusement park. Every object that existed then was hit thousands of times. So when scientists see an object with a smooth "skin," they know its surface must be relatively new—formed after collisions became less frequent.

Although Voyager pictures of Europa do not explain when or how this new surface might have formed, images from *Galileo* provide some clues. They show that Europa may contain an ocean of liquid or frozen slush beneath its icy crust. Some scientists estimate that Europa's ocean may be ten times deeper than any ocean on Earth. Water or slush oozing through cracks in Europa's icy exterior has probably refrozen to create the smooth exterior. Even more exciting, some scientists think that Europa's ocean may contain the chemicals needed for life to develop and thrive!

What makes scientists think there's an ocean on Europa? By analyzing the light emitted from the moon, researchers have known for many years that its surface is composed of water ice. They also know that if the moon's interior is warm enough, the underside of that ice could have melted to form bodies of water. When scientists viewed *Galileo*'s images, they looked closely for evidence that water existed below the moon's icy surface.

In December 1997, *Galileo* returned the first photos of a large crater called Pwyll. This crater is so shallow that its floor is nearly level with the moon's surface. Yet scientists could tell that the meteorite that caused the crater had hit hard—hard enough to plow into the interior and throw out dark streaks of material. If Europa were made of solid ice, this impact should have made a dent at least as deep as the

Grand Canyon. Thus, Pwyll Crater offered evidence that fluid beneath Europa's crust had filled the crater almost immediately, returning the surface to nearly its former level.

Images from *Galileo* also show large areas of chunky, textured surface. These regions look a lot like huge ice rafts floating on the surface

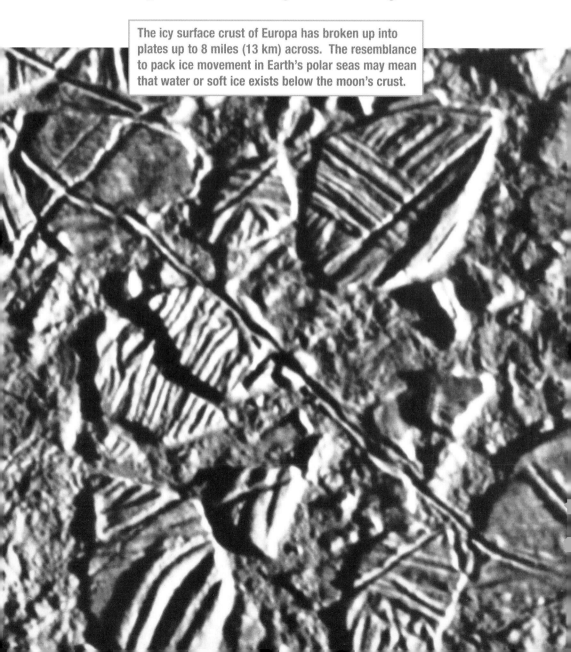

The icy surface crust of Europa has broken up into plates up to 8 miles (13 km) across. The resemblance to pack ice movement in Earth's polar seas may mean that water or soft ice exists below the moon's crust.

of an ocean. Between the chunks, scientists can discern rough, jumbled textures. Could these be areas of slush or liquid? Could the icy surface have broken open, exposed oceanic waters, and then refrozen?

In some photos, scientists have observed something even more exciting—areas that appear to be new icy crust that has formed between

In this color-enhanced photo of Europa's surface, ice mixed with rocky material is red or brown and ice is blue. The brown lines are cracks in the icy crust that have been filled by material oozing up from below.

huge, continent-sized plates of ice. Ridges and parallel grooves scar these dark, wedge-shaped regions. These markings look very similar to new crust on the Earth's seafloor, where *magma* has seeped up from the planet's interior. On Europa, it seems as though water or slushy ice, rather than magma, is breaking through the surface.

How could this world so far away from the Sun have a liquid ocean? No one is sure. Perhaps tidal tugs from Jupiter and neighboring moons stretch Europa's insides back and forth, creating heat that warms the moon's interior and melting ice that is not exposed to the coldness of space.

The pictures taken by the *Galileo* spacecraft in 1997 have transformed how scientists view Europa. If an ocean of water or ice-and-water slush exists beneath the moon's icy crust, all the elements necessary for life—heat, liquid water, and organic material introduced by meteorites—are most likely present. Perhaps one day scientists will find some simple form of life on Europa! If so, it would be the first time humans have discovered life anywhere outside Earth's cradling atmosphere!

Mystery Moon

Ganymede is the largest moon in the solar system. With a diameter of 3,268 miles (5,260 km), it outranks both Mercury and Pluto in size. Still, Ganymede is much smaller than Earth, so when *Galileo* discovered a magnetic field surrounding the moon, scientists were amazed. It is the only moon in our solar system with a magnetic field. When Ganymede's magnetic field interacts with the charged particles in solar wind, the result is a small magnetosphere that exists *within* the giant magnetosphere of Jupiter.

In this Voyager image, Ganymede's surface shows evidence of intense bombardment by meteorites, as well as some areas that have been smoothed over.

Voyager photos of Ganymede show a mysterious icy surface marked by craters, deep grooves or fractures, and tumbled blocks of ice. The spacecraft were too far away from the moon to show any details of its surface, but *Galileo* sent back dozens of close-up views. It flew as close to Ganymede as the Space Shuttle flies above Earth. As a result, scientists now know that Ganymede's surface is geologically complex.

About half of the moon's surface is dark, "dirty" ice. The other half seems to be clean, bright ice. Old impact craters pock Ganymede's surface, along with ancient volcanic deposits and other geological remnants of a much more active, far-distant past. The largest craters look oddly flattened and shallow—unlike craters seen on Earth's Moon, Mercury, and other rocky surfaces. This flattening may occur because Ganymede's surface is composed of easily degraded ice. The mountains and valleys may just evaporate or crumble away, smoothing the sharp, rugged edges of Ganymede's features.

Scientists believe that, like Europa, Ganymede may once have had an ocean below its icy crust. The moon's crust appears to have fractured, causing water volcanoes and rivers to gush out and then quickly freeze and reform the surface. However, the big moon is now frozen solid. Could simple life forms have once existed on this world too? No one knows for sure, but it is a remote possibility.

Ancient, Cratered Rock

Callisto is a bleak world that moves in an orbit 1,170,000 miles (1,885,000 km) from Jupiter. Its dark, deeply pockmarked surface reveals ancient scars gouged out by thousands of impacts. It is the oldest object ever discovered in the solar system, a primordial moon that dates back 4.5 billion years and has probably changed very little since it formed.

Callisto is larger than Earth's Moon and only a little smaller than Mercury. However, its mass is small for its size. This means that the material it is made of must be much less dense and less tightly packed than the materials that make up other worlds. Scientists believe Callisto is composed of about 60 percent iron rock and 40 percent ice.

Geologists think of Callisto as a "dead moon"—a ghost moon, frozen in time. The ripples surrounding its ancient craters appear to have remained unchanged for billions of years. *Galileo*'s close flybys

This color-enhanced image from *Voyager 2* shows that Callisto is an ancient, heavily cratered world.

have revealed a surface frosted with patches of water ice and a very thin atmosphere of oxygen. Despite this surprising similarity to Earth, most scientists agree that Callisto could never have supported life and never will.

The Outer Moons

Beyond the Galilean moons, nine more moons cut concentric paths, farther and farther from Jupiter. Their shapes are irregular and most are very small. They range in size from about 3 to 115 miles (4.8 to 185 km) in diameter and form two groups—an inner group and an outer group. The inner group orbits almost 7 million miles (11 million km) from the giant planet. The outermost satellites orbit much farther out—up to 14 million miles (22.6 million km) from Jupiter.

How Science Works: A New Moon

In July 2000, astronomers working for the Spacewatch Project in Tucson, Arizona, made an exciting announcement. The previous year, while looking for evidence of asteroids that might be on a crash course with Earth, they identified a new moon orbiting Jupiter! Surprisingly, they made their discovery using a 79-year-old, 36-inch (91-cm) telescope. The observation was confirmed in August 2000 by astronomers in Chile and France using European Space Observatory telescopes.

For now, the moon is being called S1999-J1, but when its orbit is confirmed by additional observations, it will get a new, classier name based on Jupiter's mythology theme. The new moon is an addition to the small group of farflung outer moons that travel around Jupiter in non-circular, inclined orbits.

These moons take about two Earth-years to complete one trip around the king of the planets. Like the other moons in this region, S1999-J1 was probably captured after Jupiter and its system formed. Because it is slightly red—a color common in asteroids—scientists think it may be a captured asteroid. It is only about 3 miles (4.8 km) across, making it Jupiter's smallest moon.

Moons of Jupiter

Vital Statistics

Moon	Diameter	Distance from Jupiter	Year Discovered
ADRASTEA	9.9 miles (16 km)	80,157 miles (129,000 km)	1979
AMALTHEA	162.8 miles (262 km)	112,654 miles (181,300 km)	1892
ANANKE	18.6 miles (30 km)	13,173,044 miles (21,200,000 km)	1951
CALLISTO	2,983 miles (4,800 km)	1,170,000 miles (1,885,000 km)	1610
CARME	18.6 miles (30 km)	14,042,962 miles (22,600,000 km)	1938
ELARA	46.6 miles (75 km)	7,293,020 miles (11,740,000 km)	1905
EUROPA	1,951 miles (3,140 km)	416,900 miles (670,900 km)	1610
GANYMEDE	3,268 miles (5,260 km)	664,900 miles (1,070,000 km)	1610
HIMALIA	115 miles (185 km)	7,133,328 miles (11,470,000 km)	1904
IO	2,256 miles (3,630 km)	261,970 miles (421,600 km)	1610
LEDA	9.3 miles (15 km)	6,893,479 miles (11,110,000 km)	1974
LYSITHEA	21.7 miles (35 km)	7,282,456 miles (11,710,000 km)	1938
METIS	26.7 miles (43 km)	79,535 miles (128,000 km)	1979

Vital Statistics

Moon	Diameter	Distance from Jupiter	Year Discovered
PASIPHAE	31.1 miles (50 km)	14,602,195 miles (23,500,000 km)	1908
S1999-J1	3 miles (4.8 km)	15,000,000 miles (24,000,000 km)	1999
SINOPE	21.7 miles (35 km)	14,726,469 miles (23,700,000 km)	1914
THEBE	61.5 miles (99 km)	137,882 miles (221,900 km)	1979

Many of Jupiter's outer moons may have once been asteroids or wandering meteoroids that were passing by and became caught in orbit around the big planet. Several orbit Jupiter in an east-to-west direction—the opposite direction from most orbits in the solar system.

Astronomers came up with a clever system for naming these outer moons. Those with names ending in "a"—Elara, Himalia, Leda, and Lysithea—have ordinary, west-to-east orbits. Those with names ending in "e"—Ananke, Carme, Pasiphae, and Sinope—orbit in the opposite direction, from east to west. Sinope's orbit is larger than any other known satellite's. It travels at a distance of 14,726,469 miles (23,700,000 km) from Jupiter. However, that record may be challenged by the moon first spotted in 1999 and given preliminary confirmation in 2000.

Comet Shoemaker-Levy 9 was on a collision course with Jupiter.

Chapter 7

A Colliding Comet

On the night of March 24, 1993, a history-making photograph was taken on Palomar Mountain in California. Three astronomers looking over the photographs from that night's work spotted a *short-period comet* that no one had ever noticed before. It was the ninth comet discovered by this trio—Eugene Shoemaker, Carolyn Shoemaker, and David Levy—and it was therefore named Comet Shoemaker–Levy 9.

By May 1993, astronomers realized that Comet Shoemaker-Levy 9 was heading straight for the planet Jupiter. It was on a direct collision course. Nothing like this had ever been observed before. A cosmic event this exciting probably happens only about once every 1,000 years.

After graduating from Princeton University in New Jersey, Eugene Shoemaker began working for the United States Geological Survey (USGS). At first, he spent most of his time searching for uranium deposits. Then he began to investigate nuclear craters and compare them with Meteor Crater in Arizona. That project made him start to think about impact craters on other worlds, such as the Moon.

Gene wanted to be an astronaut, but health conditions prevented that. However, beginning in 1961, he helped train the Apollo astronauts in the basics of Moon geology, so that they would know what to look for when they got there. He also taught geology at California Technology Institute in Pasadena, California, and helped asteroid specialist Eleanor Helin set up a project that searched the sky for near-Earth asteroids.

In 1980, Gene's wife, Carolyn, began working with Eleanor Helin. This is how the Shoemakers, together with David Levy, discovered Comet Shoemaker-Levy 9 in 1993. Three years later, during one of their annual trips to Australia to examine impact craters, the Shoemakers' car collided head-on with another vehicle in the middle of Australia's Tanami Desert. Gene was killed instantly. Carolyn was injured and hospitalized, but later recovered.

In 1999, a little spacecraft named *Lunar Prospector* visited the Moon to explore lunar geology and map the Moon. As a tribute to Gene Shoemaker, it carried 1 ounce (28 grams) of his ashes in a cylinder deeply embedded in the spacecraft.

David Levy (left), Eugene Shoemaker (center), and Carolyn Shoemaker (right) celebrate the "smashing success" of Comet Shoemaker-Levy 9.

In this illustration, the white lines represent the orbital paths of planets, and the red line shows the elliptical orbit of a comet.

Most comets have very large, elliptical orbits that loop far out to the edge of the solar system and zoom in to curve around the Sun. While some do have shorter orbits, it is unusual for a comet to become trapped by Jupiter's gravitational field. Apparently, Comet Shoemaker-Levy 9 had passed close to Jupiter several times. Each time, the giant planet had robbed some of the comet's momentum. Eventually, the comet was pulled out of its long, elliptical orbit and began to orbit Jupiter.

As scientists continued to study Comet Shoemaker-Levy 9, they learned that on July 7, 1992, the comet came so close to Jupiter that it had shattered into many fragments. Jupiter's immense gravitational field had tugged and racked the fragile ball of ice and rock until it flew apart.

Torn to Pieces

In recent years, astronomers have realized that few comets or asteroids are cohesive, tightly packed objects. Usually, they have been whacked around over and over as they sail through the solar system—often disintegrating and reassembling. Some may never have fused into a single body in the first place. So they are roving "rubble piles," as Eugene and Carolyn Shoemaker once put it.

Computer simulations show that loosely assembled objects composed of chunks of rock and ice may come apart if they get too close to the gravitational field of an object—even an object the size of Earth. When Comet Shoemaker-Levy 9 passed so close to Jupiter in 1992, it didn't have a chance. Evidence is mounting that this kind of breakup is much more common than astronomers previously thought. Studies show that double craters found on Earth could not have been caused by fragmentation after an asteroid or comet hit the atmosphere. Instead, the object must have split first, and then hit.

By the time Comet Shoemaker-Levy 9 was identified on photographic plates, it was bar-shaped and had several tails. Two wings of dust extended from each end of the bar. Within a few weeks, an extremely powerful telescope had captured an image of the comet revealing that the "bar" actually consisted of a series of *nuclei* that looked like a string of pearls.

In this photo, Comet Shoemaker-Levy 9 resembles a string of pearls.

Comet Shoemaker-Levy 9 had crumbled into pieces—twenty-one pieces at best count. Tidal stress had torn it apart. When it became obvious that this string of ice chunks was headed straight for Jupiter, astronomers began to marshal their resources to record the spectacular event from every possible angle.

Countdown to Impact

On July 12, 1994, the *Hubble Space Telescope* observed dramatic changes in Jupiter's magnetosphere. For about 2 minutes, *Hubble* detected a large quantity of magnesium—one of the major elements in comet dust. About 18 minutes later, a significant change took place in the light reflected from the dust particles in Comet Shoemaker-Levy 9. A comet fragment had entered the inner realm of Jupiter.

Some astronomers expected the comet fragments to shatter into even smaller pieces shortly before impact. They thought the giant planet's huge tidal forces would stretch the pieces until they disinte-

Shortly before impact, the comet's fragments stretched across the sky.

grated. However, just 10 hours before impact, the *Hubble Space Telescope* took a stunning image of the comet's fragments stretched out in a long row, each one distinct and solid. Most astronomers conclude from this evidence that the pieces did not disintegrate. The freight train of fragments hit Jupiter one "car" at a time—moving at a speed of about 37 miles (60 km) per second. The first pieces hit on July 16, 1994, followed by four more on July 17. A few more fragments crashed into the big planet's atmosphere each day for 6 days.

As each fragment hit Jupiter's atmosphere, it threw up a titanic fireball. Some of the fireballs had temperatures as high as 31,940°F (18,000°C). As each piece struck the planet, brightness in the area increased by as much as 15 percent.

Scientists think the fireballs represented only a small fraction of the total energy output from the blasts. Most of that energy was probably absorbed by Jupiter's atmosphere. When comet fragments containing high proportions of ice hit the planet, they sent plumes of water spewing into space.

Within 30 minutes, huge black clouds began to form where the fireballs had been. These dark spots looked like pancakes in Jupiter's atmosphere. Some measured up to 6,214 miles (10,000 km) across. At least one cloud was large enough to swallow up the entire Earth. The blemishes were still visible months after the collision, although the planet's constant easterly and westerly winds soon curled their edges. Eventually, the scars faded from Jupiter's complexion.

The *Hubble Space Telescope's* Faint Object Spectrograph showed a high content of sulfur-bearing compounds in the mysterious dark

The *Hubble Space Telescope* captured this image of two impact sites, shortly after the first few Shoemaker-Levy 9 fragments hit.

clouds. Most of these compounds seemed to disperse within a few days, but the ammonia in the spots took several months to dissipate. The dark areas also contained silicon, magnesium, and iron—substances not found on Jupiter. They must have come from the comet fragments.

The impact of one fragment known as "K" created spectacular aurorae in a different location from Jupiter's usual light shows. Astronomers believe that when K hit Jupiter's atmosphere, it created an electromagnetic disturbance in the planet's magnetosphere.

Observing a Smash Hit

Comet Shoemaker-Levy 9 smashed into the night side of Jupiter—the side turned away from Earth at the time. So Earth-based astronomers had no hope of seeing the event directly. However, both professional and amateur astronomers found ways to observe its effects.

Astronomers watched the edge of Jupiter's disk for signs of the impact. They observed the dark spots in the cloud tops as the globe rotated and the area that had been struck came into view. They also used instruments to measure changes in Jupiter's magnetosphere. Never before in the history of astronomy had so many telescopes and instruments been trained on one single event.

Voyager 2, *Galileo*, and *Ulysses* also helped scientists study the collision. *Voyager 2* had finished its missions to Jupiter, Saturn, Uranus, and Neptune long before and was on its way out of the solar system. It was 3,852,500,000 miles (6,200,000,000 km) away. Nevertheless, the spacecraft used its ultraviolet spectrometer and planetary radio astronomy instrument to detect, time, and measure impact-related emissions from Jupiter.

Galileo, the only direct witness of the cosmic impacts, took this image.

Galileo was the only spacecraft with a direct view of the nightside areas where the comet pieces hit. Even though it was 150 million miles (240 million km) from Jupiter, *Galileo* was close enough to see the events as well as the best Earth-based telescopes would have seen them if the collision were visible from Earth.

At the time of the collision, *Ulysses* was making a swing past the southern pole of the Sun, but it could see Jupiter well from there, and it did its part. Scientists used the spacecraft's combined radio and plasma wave instrument to search for radio signals caused by the Shoemaker-Levy impacts.

The series of collisions was tremendously exciting, but it was also sobering. The impacts released more energy into Jupiter's atmosphere than the energy of all Earth's nuclear arsenals combined. They had an enormous effect on the giant planet's atmosphere, and the clear message for Earth was: If it can happen on Jupiter, it can happen here too. It was, as one astronomer put it, "The astronomical event of the century."

How Science Works: Learning from Catastrophe

Astronomers can see the cloud tops of Jupiter, but the rest of the giant planet's atmosphere is difficult to see or analyze. However, a rare opportunity to see inside the planet came when fragments of Comet Shoemaker-Levy 9 plowed into Jupiter.

The *Hubble Space Telescope*'s ultraviolet observations showed the scattering of very fine impact debris particles high in Jupiter's atmosphere. *Hubble* was able to track these suspended particles as they moved down to lower altitudes, providing a sort of map of wind patterns inside the planet.

At higher altitudes, the winds appear to move between the planet's poles and the equator. The driving force is provided by the same high-energy particles that cause Jupiter's impressive aurorae. As the impact debris moved into lower levels of the atmosphere, their movement was controlled by east-west winds created by Jupiter's own internal heat.

This artist's conception shows the *Cassini-Huygens* spacecraft approaching Saturn's big moon Titan, with the planet in the background.

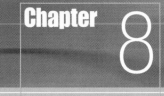

Chapter 8

Unanswered Questions

Four brief visits to Jupiter by the Pioneers and the Voyagers, a much longer tour of the Jupiter system by the Galileo spacecraft, and short encounters by *Ulysses* and *Cassini-Huygens* have not quenched our thirst to know more about the king of the planets. The more scientists learn, the more questions they want to ask. When it comes to Jupiter, many mysteries remain.

Is Jupiter's core solid or liquid? Why is the Great Red Spot so red? How deep does this huge storm system go? Why is there only one red spot? What force has caused the Great Red Spot to swirl so endlessly, over the course of centuries?

Could some microscopic form of life currently exist in the frozen slush that makes up Europa's oceans? Could life have once existed on

This compuer-generated montage of images shows Jupiter and its four largest moons: Io (second right), Europa (just to the right of Jupiter), Ganymede (far right), and Callisto (foreground).

Ganymede? Is there some unusual life form living in the upper and warmer layers of the clouds of the giant planet itself?

How is Jupiter's magnetosphere affected by the ebb and flow of the solar wind? What are the dynamics of the interaction between the nested magnetospheres of Jupiter and Ganymede?

These questions and more still teem in the minds of planetary scientists. *Galileo's* visit to Jupiter and the Galilean moons was a stunning success, but now many scientists want to send a special spacecraft to Europa. They hope that such a mission can answer one of the biggest questions of the century: Does life exist elsewhere in the universe?

Many scientists have recently started to think that Jupiter may play a major role in making life possible on Earth. As the collision of Comet Shoemaker-Levy 9 showed us, Jupiter's enormous gravitational field has the power to pull objects out of their orbits. Perhaps Earth has had so few cataclysmic strikes because Jupiter sweeps the area clean of "loose cannons" that might otherwise crash into our planet. Does the giant planet protect its neighbors? If so, the study of Jupiter takes on new meaning. One thing is certain. The more we find out about Jupiter and its large family, the better we will understand the forces that affect our region of the universe.

Missions to Jupiter

Vital Statistics

Spacecraft	Type of Mission	Year of Arrival	Sponsor
PIONEER 10	Flyby	1973	NASA
PIONEER 11	Flyby	1974	NASA
VOYAGER 1	Flyby	1979	NASA
VOYAGER 2	Flyby	1979	NASA
ULYSSES	Flyby	1992	NASA/ESA
GALILEO	Orbiter/Probe	1995	NASA
CASSINI-HUYGENS	Flyby	2000	NASA/ESA

Exploring Jupiter: A Timeline

364 B.C. — Gan De, a Chinese astronomer, observes a body that astronomers now think must have been Ganymede.

1610 — Galileo Galilei makes his first observation of Jupiter's four largest moons.

1664 — British chemist and physicist Robert Hooke discovers Jupiter's Great Red Spot and accurately describes the planet's rotation.

1665 — Giovanni Domenico Cassini measures the rate of Jupiter's rotation.

1866 — Daniel Kirkwood, an American astronomer, shows that Jupiter's gravity influences the orbits of asteroids in the asteroid belt.

1892 — The moon Amalthea is discovered.

1904 — The moon Himalia is discovered.

1905 — The moon Elara is discovered.

1908 — The moon Pasiphae is discovered.

1914	The moon Sinope is discovered.
1938	The moons Carme and Lysithea are discovered.
1951	The moon Ananke is discovered.
1955	Scientists detect radio signals from Jupiter.
1957	The former Soviet Union (USSR) launches the first artificial satellite, *Sputnik 1*, into Earth orbit.
1958	The United States launches its first satellite, *Explorer 1*.
1973	*Pioneer 10* becomes the first spacecraft to fly by Jupiter and its moons, providing the first pictures taken from space.
1974	The moon Leda is discovered.
	Pioneer 11 flies by Jupiter and its moons and sends back more images.
1979	*Voyager 1* and *Voyager 2* visit Jupiter and its moons and send back the first detailed images.

1989	— The Galileo spacecraft is launched to visit Jupiter and its four largest moons—Io, Europa, Ganymede, and Callisto.
1992	— *Ulysses* passes by Jupiter and uses the planet's gravity to reach its ultimate target—the Sun.
1997	— Cassini-Huygens mission heads for Saturn and Titan. On its way, it studies Jupiter briefly.
1999	— Scientists discover a seventeenth moon orbiting Jupiter.

asteroid—a piece of rocky debris left over from the formation of the solar system. Most asteroids orbit the Sun in a belt between Mars and Jupiter.

asteroid belt—the region between Mars and Jupiter, where most asteroids orbit

aurora (pl. aurorae)—a display of light caused by interaction between charged particles and a planet's magnetic field

comet—a small ball of rock and ice that usually travels toward the sun in a long orbit that originates on the remote outer edge of the solar system

crater—a rimmed basin or depression on the surface of a planet or moon caused by the impact of a meteorite

density—the amount of a substance in a given volume

electromagnetic radiation—one or more of a range of waves and frequencies of energy that make up the electromagnetic spectrum. Radar and infrared rays are at one end of the spectrum and have very long wavelengths. Visible light is about in the middle. At the other end of the spectrum are types of radiation with such short wavelengths that they are invisible to humans, including ultraviolet (UV) waves, X-rays, and gamma rays. The frequency of radio

waves ranges from about 10 kilohertz to 300,000 megahertz and can be heard by humans.

flyby—a mission that takes a spacecraft past a planet to make observations, but doesn't involve orbiting or landing

gravitational field—the region around an object that is affected by its gravitational pull

gravity—the force that pulls things toward the center of a large object in space, such as a planet or moon

gravity assist—a maneuver in which a spacecraft circles a body in space and uses the object's gravitational pull to increase its acceleration

hypothesis—a tentative scientific explanation drawn from the most reliable data available

magma—hot, soft rock below the surface of a planet or moon

magnetic field—the area surrounding a magnet that is affected by the magnet's attractive force. Some planets have magnetic properties and, therefore, have a magnetic field.

magnetism—a force that enables some objects to attract or repel certain other objects even when they are not in contact

magnetosphere—the vast area around a planet that is filled with electrically charged particles and electromagnetic radiation; it is caused by the interaction of the planet's magnetic field and the solar wind

mass—the amount of matter an object contains

meteoroid—a rocky or metallic object of relatively small size, usually once part of a comet or asteroid

nebula (pl. nebulae)—a primitive cloud of gases and dust from which stars and planetary systems are born

nuclear fusion—a process that takes place in the core of the Sun and other stars, releasing enormous energy when two atoms of hydrogen combine to form helium

nucleus (pl. nuclei)—the round main body of a comet

planetesimal—the precursor of a planet

radius—the distance from the outer edge of a round object, such as a planet, to its center

satellite—a natural or human-made object that orbits another body, such as a planet or an asteroid

short-period comet—a comet that does not to travel to the edge of the solar system because it is influenced by the gravitational field of one of the planets

solar wind—the rush of electrically charged particles emitted by the Sun

tidal force—the difference between the force of gravity on the near and far sides of an object in space

ultraviolet rays—radiation with wavelengths just shorter than violet light; "black light" is a form of UV radiation.

volume—the amount of three-dimensional space occupied by an object

To Find Out More

The news from space changes fast, so it's always a good idea to check the copyright date on books, CD-ROMs, and video tapes to make sure that you are getting up-to-date information. One good place to look for current information from NASA is U.S. government depository libraries. There are several in each state.

Books

Campbell, Ann Jeanette. *The New York Public Library Amazing Space: A Book of Answers for Kids.* New York: John Wiley & Sons, 1997.

Dickinson, Terence. *Other Worlds: A Beginner's Guide to Planets and Moons.* Willowdale, Ontario: Firefly Books, 1995.

Gustafson, John. *Planets, Moons and Meteors.* New York: Julian Messner, 1992.

Hartmann, William K. and Don Miller. *The Grand Tour.* New York: Workman Publishing, 1993.

Vogt, Gregory L. *The Solar System Facts and Exploration.* Scientific American Sourcebooks. New York: Twenty-First Century Books, 1995.

CD-ROMs

Beyond Planet Earth, Discovery Channel School, P.O. Box 970, Oxon Hill, MD 20750-0970.
An interactive journey to the planets, including Jupiter. Includes video footage and more than 200 still photographs.

Organizations and Online Sites

These organizations and online sites are good sources of information about Jupiter and the rest of the solar system. Many of the online sites listed below are NASA sites, with links to many other interesting sources of information about the solar system. You can also sign up to receive NASA news on many subjects via e-mail.

Astronomical Society of the Pacific
http://www.aspsky.org/
390 Ashton Avenue
San Francisco, CA 94112

The Astronomy Café
http://www2.ari.net/home/odenwald/cafe.html
This site answers questions and offers news and articles relating to astronomy and space. It is maintained by astronomer and NASA scientist Sten Odenwald.

Galileo Mission

http://www.jpl.nasa.gov/galileo/

This site describes the details of the Galileo mission and has a multitude of images and animations of Jupiter and its moons.

NASA Ask a Space Scientist

http://image.gsfc.nasa.gov/poetry/ask/askmag.html#list

Take a look at the Interactive Page where NASA scientists answer your questions about astronomy, space, and space missions. The site also has access to archives and fact sheets.

NASA Newsroom

http://www.nasa.gov/newsinfo/newsroom.html

This site features NASA's latest press releases, status reports, and fact sheets. It includes a news archive with past reports and a search button for the NASA Web site. You can even sign up for e-mail versions of all NASA press releases.

The Nine Planets: A Multimedia Tour of the Solar System

http://www.seds.org/nineplanet/nineplanets/nineplanets.html

This site has excellent material on the planets, including Jupiter. It was created and is maintained by the Students for the Exploration and Development of Space, University of Arizona.

Planetary Missions
http://nssdc.gsfc.nasa.gov/planetary/projects.html
At this site, you'll find NASA links to all current and past missions. It's a one-stop shopping center to a wealth of information.

The Planetary Society
http://www.planetary.org/
65 North Catalina Avenue
Pasadena, CA 91106-2301

Sky Online
http://www.skypub.com
This is the Web site for *Sky and Telescope* magazine and other publications of Sky Publishing Corporation. You'll find a good weekly news section on general space and astronomy news. The site also has tips for amateur astronomers as well as a nice selection of links. A list of science museums, planetariums, and astronomy clubs organized by state can help you locate nearby places to visit.

Welcome to the Planets
http://pds.jpl.nasa.gov/planets/
This tour of the solar system has lots of pictures and information. The site was created and is maintained by the California Institute of Technology for NASA/Jet Propulsion Laboratory.

Windows to the Universe

http://windows.ivv.nasa.gov/

This NASA site, developed by the University of Michigan, includes sections on "Our Planet," "Our Solar System," "Space Missions," and "Kids' Space." Choose from presentation levels of beginner, intermediate, or advanced.

Places to Visit

Check the Internet (*www.skypub.com* is a good place to start), your local visitor's center, or phone directory for planetariums and science museums near you. Here are a few suggestions:

Ames Research Center

Moffett Field, CA 94035

http://www.arc.nasa.gov/

Located near Mountain View and Sunnyvale on the San Francisco Peninsula, Ames Research Center welcomes visitors. This is the branch of NASA that sponsored Pioneer Venus and heads the search for extraterrestrial life. Drop-in visitors are welcome and admission is free.

Exploratorium

3601 Lyon Street
San Francisco, CA 94123

http://www.exploratorium.edu/

You'll find internationally acclaimed interactive science exhibits, including astronomy subjects.

Jet Propulsion Laboratory (JPL)
4800 Oak Grove Drive
Pasadena, CA 91109
http://www.jpl.nasa.gov/faq/#tour
JPL is the primary mission center for most NASA planetary missions.
Tours are available once or twice a week by arrangement.

National Air and Space Museum
7th and Independence Ave., S.W.
Washington, DC 20560
http://www.nasm.edu/NASMDOCS/VISIT/
This museum, located on the National Mall west of the Capitol building, has all kinds of interesting exhibits.

Bold numbers indicate illustrations.

Ray Spangenburg and **Kit Moser** are a husband-and-wife writing team specializing in science and technology. They have written 38 books and more than 100 articles, including a 5-book series on the history of science and a 4-book series on the history of space exploration. As journalists, they covered NASA and related science activities for many years. They have flown on NASA's Kuiper Airborne Observatory, covered stories at the Deep Space Network in the Mojave Desert, and experienced zero-gravity on experimental NASA flights out of NASA Ames Research Center. They live in Carmichael, California, with their two dogs, Mencken (a Sharpei mix) and F. Scott Fitz (a Boston terrier).